VOLUME 14

Families Are Forev[e]

TINY TALKS

VOLUME 14

Families Are Forever

TINY TALKS

Heidi Doxey

Illustrated by Corey Egbert

CFI
An Imprint of Cedar Fort, Inc.
Springville, Utah

ISBN: 978-1-4621-1357-6

Published by CFI, an imprint of Cedar Fort, Inc.
2373 W. 700 S., Springville, Utah, 84663
www.cedarfort.com

Front cover design by Corey Egbert
Back cover design by Shawnda T. Craig
Cover design © 2013 Lyle Mortimer
Edited and typeset by Emily S. Chambers

Printed in the United States of America

10 9 8 7 6 5 4 3 2 1

For Nani, who keeps me crazy. —H.D.

For Oliver. —C.E.

Contents

Agost

Sep

Oct

Nov

Dic

Introduction

This year in Primary, we will learn about how families can be together forever. This is one of the most important parts of Heavenly Father's plan of happiness. Knowing that our families can be sealed forever changes how we feel about our families and how we treat them. We try to love each other more and work harder to be kind because we know we will be with each other eternally, if we are righteous. Even though every family is different, each one is important to Heavenly Father. He wants you to make good choices your whole life so you can be with your own family forever.

This book is a great resource when you need to write a talk for Primary—especially at the last minute—but it can also be used in family home evenings, sharing time, your Primary class, or for individual study. Discussing the principles and eternal truths in this book will bring you closer together as a family.

Each talk includes five different elements: a story, a

scripture, a visual aid, a list of suggested illustrations, and a thought question.

STORY

Heavenly Father has given us many examples in the scriptures and in our own lives that illustrate how important families are and how we can be with our families forever. We need to practice applying these examples to our own lives. This is a necessary skill for salvation and one children can learn early. The stories in this book come from the scriptures and from real life. As you read them, encourage your children to think of other stories from the scriptures that incorporate the topics in the lesson. Nephi tells us that we need to "liken all scriptures unto us," and that this will benefit us and help us to learn from them (1 Nephi 19:23). Likewise, when your children give talks, always encourage them to make the talk personal by sharing how the principles they are speaking about apply to them. Encourage them to bear a simple testimony at the end of their talks.

VISUAL AID

In addition to a story, each talk includes a reference to a visual aid from the Gospel Art Book (GAB). This resource is available online and can be an excellent help. If you wish to purchase your own copy of the Gospel Art Book, it is available through Church Distribution Services. Another option is to have your children illustrate their talks.

LIST OF ILLUSTRATIONS

With each talk, you will find a list of suggested illustrations that complement the story. This is especially useful for children who are too young to read the talk themselves. By having your children color their own pictures of the things discussed in the talk, you will help them remember the concepts they learned as you also encourage them to share their talents. Some of these illustrations are repeated in other talks, so you may want to keep your pictures handy to use again later. In this way, your family can build your own personal art kit to use in family home evening and other settings. This will be a treasured resource and will bring back many good memories in years to come.

As a family night variation, before the lesson begins, you could have your children take turns drawing the illustrations while everyone guesses what the picture is. Once all the pictures have been drawn, have the children guess the topic of the lesson by looking at the pictures they've drawn.

THOUGHT QUESTION

Finally, each talk includes a thought question. These questions are specifically geared toward older children and teenagers, though, with a little parental prompting, they can be appropriate for young children. These questions will help you to include your whole family in discussions and talk preparation. They can help you all to delve a little deeper into the doctrine behind each story. As you discuss these topics, make sure your children have a chance to express their thoughts. You may be surprised by how much they have already learned about the gospel.

SONG IDEAS

Another resource is the list of song ideas at the end of this book. These songs are from the *Children's Songbook*. For each tiny talk, you will find at least one song that corresponds to the themes and ideas presented that week. For young children especially, music can be a wonderful way to reinforce and expand on key doctrinal concepts. Learning these songs when they are young will give your children a solid foundation to rely on for years to come. Even if your own musical abilities are limited, you will find joy in singing with your children and in sharing with them the precious gospel truths contained in the lyrics. You can find audio and lyrics for most of these songs online at lds.org/music.

I hope you will enjoy this book and find many uses for it throughout the year. I am so grateful to all the Church leaders and friends who have taught and encouraged me. And I'm especially grateful for my family. They are wonderful examples to me, and I am so excited to spend eternity with them.

CHAPTER 1

HEAVENLY FATHER WANTS ME *to* LIVE *with* HIM AGAIN

"For God so loved the world, that he gave his only begotten Son, that whosoever believeth in him should not perish, but have everlasting life." —John 3:16

1. GOD IS MY FATHER, AND I CAN BE LIKE HIM

SCRIPTURE

Ye are gods; and all of you are children of the most High.
—Psalm 82:6

VISUAL AID

GAB 90
"The First Vision"

ILLUSTRATION IDEAS

An airplane, a boy, a pilot, Heavenly Father

Spencer's dad is a pilot. He flies planes all around the world. Spencer loves to watch his dad push the buttons that make the plane start up, move forward, and fly into the air. Flying an airplane is tricky, but Spencer's dad has practiced flying a lot. Now his dad knows how to fly safely and keep the airplane going the right way. Someday Spencer wants to be a pilot, just like his dad.

Spencer also has a Heavenly Father. Our Heavenly Father can do lots of things. He can create worlds and rule the whole universe. He learned how to do this by practicing and working hard. He wants us to learn all the things he has learned and become like him.

When we choose the right, we become more like our Heavenly Father. We can learn and practice making good choices now so that someday we will know everything our Heavenly Father knows and be able to do all the wonderful things he can do.

Thought Question: What does it mean to have divine potential?

2. JESUS IS MY SAVIOR, AND HE HELPS ME BECOME BETTER

Here on earth, nothing stays perfect forever. The flowers that come in springtime are gone by the fall. The snowmen made in the winter have to melt. And no matter how many times we clean our rooms, they always get messy again.

People are the same way. None of us can be perfect. We can try our best, but there is no way we can become perfect on our own. Heavenly Father knows we can't do it alone. That's why he sent his Son to help us. Jesus came to earth to set an example for us. He also died for us. This was called the Atonement. The Atonement makes it possible for us to become perfect. When we make a mistake, we can repent and the Atonement will make it better.

Jesus and Heavenly Father love us. They want us to become perfect so we can live with them again someday.

Thought Question: How does the Atonement affect your everyday life?

SCRIPTURE

Yea, come unto Christ, and be perfected in him.
—Moroni 10:32

VISUAL AID

GAB 57
"The Crucifixion"

ILLUSTRATION IDEAS

Flowers, a snowman, a messy room, Heavenly Father, Jesus

3. JESUS SHOWS US THE RIGHT WAY

SCRIPTURE

And the Lord went before them by day in a pillar of a cloud . . . and by night in a pillar of fire, to give them light; to go by day and night.
—Exodus 13:21

VISUAL AID

GAB 13
"Moses and the Burning Bush"

ILLUSTRATION IDEAS

Moses, the Israelites, a pillar of cloud, a pillar of fire, Jesus

Moses had a hard job to do. He needed to lead his people, the Israelites, all the way from Egypt to the Promised Land. God knew that Moses would need help, so he gave Moses and the Israelites some special signs that would show them the right way to go. During the day, God gave the Israelites a pillar of cloud that led them in the right direction. And at night, a pillar of fire lighted their way.

Today we don't have pillars of fire or clouds to show us which way to go. But we do have a special kind of light that comes from Jesus. It is called the Light of Christ. Whenever we need to make a choice, the Light of Christ helps us to remember what Jesus did. We can always use the Light of Christ to follow Jesus and do what he would do. That is the way we stay safe on our journey back to Heavenly Father.

Thought Question: When you need to make a choice, how can you know what Jesus would do?

4. IF I FOLLOW JESUS, HE WILL LEAD ME BACK TO HEAVENLY FATHER

Lots of things make Jacob happy. He's happy when he gets to go to the park. He's happy when he eats fruit snacks. And he's always happy to go swimming or play in the water. It's good to be happy. There's a verse in the scriptures that tells us that Heavenly Father and Jesus created us so that we could have joy.

Things like parks and fruit snacks can make us happy for a little while, but Jesus knows what will make us happy forever. He knows that we will only be happy forever if we can return to live with our Heavenly Father someday. Heavenly Father lives in a beautiful place called heaven. It is a place where we can feel peace and love. But the only way to get to heaven is to follow Jesus Christ. If we try our best, Jesus leads us step-by-step. He shows us what to do and how to act. He will lead each of us back to heaven where we can be happy forever.

Thought Question: How can you focus your life on things that will make you happy, both now and eternally?

SCRIPTURE

And men are, that they might have joy.
—2 Nephi 2:25

VISUAL AID

GAB 84
"Jesus Blesses the Nephite Children"

ILLUSTRATION IDEAS

A boy, a park, fruit snacks, a swimming pool, Jesus, Heaven, Heavenly Father, a smile

CHAPTER 2

I Can FOLLOW HEAVENLY FATHER'S Plan

"O how great the plan of our God!" —2 Nephi 9:13

1. HEAVENLY FATHER'S PLAN IS FOR ME

SCRIPTURE

I will go and do the things which the Lord hath commanded.
—1 Nephi 3:7

VISUAL AID

GAB 37
"Calling of the Fishermen"

ILLUSTRATION IDEAS

Peter, a boat, a fish, Jesus, the earth, the scriptures

After Jesus died, many of his apostles weren't sure what to do. Peter and some of the other apostles decided to go fishing like they had done before they started following Jesus. Then Jesus appeared to them and told them that they needed to stick to his plan. Jesus said that Peter's mission was not to fish, but to lead the Church and share the gospel with the people around him.

Jesus has a plan and a mission for you too. Before you were born, Jesus presented the plan of salvation. This plan allows us to return to Heavenly Father after we die. We chose to follow the plan of salvation and come to earth. Now that we are here, each of us has a special mission to perform as we follow the plan of salvation. We can find out what our mission is by reading the scriptures, praying, and listening to the still, small voice.

Thought Question: Do you know what your special mission is? If so, how do you plan to accomplish it?

2. JESUS CREATED THIS EARTH TO BE MY HOME

Have you ever seen a beaver dam? It takes beavers a lot of work to make a dam. They have to use their teeth to chop down trees and branches. Then they drag the wood back and put it in place with mud. It takes a long time, but once the beavers finish, they have something beautiful and useful.

Heavenly Father wanted to make a beautiful and useful home for his children. Long before we were born, he commanded Jesus to create this world. Jesus worked hard. He knew we would need lots of things here on earth. We would need the sun, the moon, water, land, plants, animals, and many other things. He created all of these for us so we would have a beautiful place to call home. When we see the beautiful things around us, we should remember who made them and give thanks to Heavenly Father and Jesus for creating the earth.

Thought Question: Has Heavenly Father created other worlds besides ours?

SCRIPTURE

Behold, the Lord hath created the earth that it should be inhabited; and he hath created his children that they should possess it.
—1 Nephi 17:36

VISUAL AID

GAB 3
"The Earth"

ILLUSTRATION IDEAS

A beaver, the earth, the sun, water, planets, animals, Jesus

3. JESUS CREATED MY BODY TO LOOK LIKE HEAVENLY FATHER

SCRIPTURE

In the day that God created man, in the likeness of God made he him; In the image of his own body, male and female, created he them and blessed them.
—Moses 6:8–9

VISUAL AID

GAB 116
"Christ and Children from around the World"

ILLUSTRATION IDEAS

A girl dancing, a bike, Heavenly Father, Jesus, a group of people, a heart

Adalee likes to dance. She has taken lessons since she was little. When she dances, Adalee feels excited and happy. She loves to move her body to the music and create something that other people can watch. It takes a lot of energy to dance. Adalee is grateful that she has a body so she can dance, run, jump, ride her bike, and do all of the other things she likes to do.

Each of us has a body. Our bodies were created by Heavenly Father and Jesus. All of our bodies are a little bit different. Some people have dark hair, and others have light hair. Some people are tall, and others are short. But each of us has a body that looks like our Heavenly Father and like Jesus. They created us to look like them because we are all children of God. When we take good care of our bodies, we show Heavenly Father how much we love him and how grateful we are for the bodies he gave us.

Thought Question: Why do you think Heavenly Father made all of our bodies different?

10

4. AGENCY MEANS I GET TO CHOOSE

Jonah had a choice to make. The Lord asked Jonah to visit the people in Nineveh and tell them that they needed to repent. But Jonah didn't want to do that. Instead Jonah chose to get into a boat and go to a different city. On the way, a storm started. The other people on the ship threw Jonah overboard, and he was swallowed up by a big fish. When the fish put Jonah back on land, Jonah had to make a choice again. This time Jonah chose the right. He went to Nineveh.

Every day we get to make choices, just like Jonah. We can choose to follow the Lord and do what he wants, or we can choose to do whatever we want to do instead. Even if we choose to do something bad, Heavenly Father will never keep us from making choices. He has given us all the gift to choose. This gift is called "agency." Agency lets us learn and grow. Without agency, we would never be able to make all the good choices that will someday lead us back to our Heavenly Father.

Thought Question: Why did Heavenly Father want us to be able to make choices, even if they're bad?

SCRIPTURE

When my soul fainted within me I remembered the Lord: and my prayer came in unto thee, into thine holy temple. —Jonah 2:7

VISUAL AID

GAB 27
"Jonah"

ILLUSTRATION IDEAS

Jonah, a boat, a big fish, Jesus, Heavenly Father

CHAPTER 3

JESUS WILL HELP Me RETURN to HEAVENLY FATHER

"We have seen and do testify that the Father sent the Son to be the Saviour of the world." —1 John 4:14

1. I CAN KNOW ABOUT JESUS FOR MYSELF

SCRIPTURE

Josiah was eight years old when he began to reign . . . and he did that which was right in the sight of the Lord.
—2 Chronicles 34:1–2

VISUAL AID

GAB 65
"Jesus at the Door"

ILLUSTRATION IDEAS

King Josiah, the scriptures, Jesus, a smile

King Josiah was a young king. He started to rule when he was only eight years old. He wanted to make sure his people were doing what Jesus wanted them to do. So he decided to study the scriptures. As he did, he discovered that some of the things his people had been doing for a long time were not right. King Josiah knew it would not be easy to change. But now that he knew about Jesus for himself, he could not keep doing what was wrong. With King Josiah's help, the people changed and followed Jesus.

Just like King Josiah, you can find out about Jesus for yourself. One way to do this is by studying the scriptures. You should also pray and keep the commandments. When you do these things, you will find out for yourself what Jesus wants you to do. It doesn't matter if you are old or young. Jesus loves you. He wants you to learn about him so that someday you can become as happy as he is.

Thought Question: Which particular scriptures could you study to help you learn more about Jesus?

2. JESUS HELPS ME REPENT AND BE CLEAN

Grant loves to play in the sandbox. But sometimes instead of building sand castles or digging holes, all Grant wants to do is throw the sand around. This makes a big mess. When Grant throws sand, it gets stuck in his hair, on his clothes, and even in between his toes. Then Grant's mommy always makes him take a bath to get all the sand off of him so he can be clean again.

When our bodies get dirty, we need to take baths. Sometimes our spirits can get dirty too. This happens when we do something wrong or make a mistake. Jesus knows how to make our spirits clean again. He wants us to tell him when we do wrong so that he can help us to be clean. This is called confessing our sins. Then Jesus wants us to forsake our sins. That means that we promise never to make that mistake again. When we confess and forsake our sins, we show Jesus that we want to be clean and happy just like he is.

Thought Question: What happens if you make the same mistake again after you have repented?

SCRIPTURE

Who shall stand in his holy place? He that hath clean hands and a pure heart.
—Psalm 24:3–4

VISUAL AID

GAB 35
"John the Baptist Baptizing Jesus"

ILLUSTRATION IDEAS

A boy, a sandbox, a bathtub, Jesus

3. SOMEDAY I WILL BE RESURRECTED, LIKE JESUS WAS

SCRIPTURE

But there is a resurrection, therefore the grave hath no victory, and the sting of death is swallowed up in Christ.
—Mosiah 16:8

VISUAL AID

GAB 59
"Mary and the Resurrected Jesus Christ"

ILLUSTRATION IDEAS

Jesus, the sun, a sunset, a sunrise

Jesus is like the sun. He gives us light so we can see. He helps us feel warm and happy inside. And Jesus is like the sun in another way. Every night, we watch the sun go down. And every morning, the sun comes back up again. When Jesus died, it was like the sun going down. Many people who knew and loved Jesus were sad. They did not understand that he would be resurrected. It was like they thought the sun would never rise again.

Then three days later, Jesus did rise again. His body and spirit were joined together. His friends were happy. They knew Jesus had overcome death. Because Jesus was resurrected, each of us will be resurrected too. Our bodies and spirits will be joined together forever in a new, perfect resurrected body. Each time we see the sun, we can remember how Jesus was resurrected, and how someday we will be resurrected too.

Thought Question: Will everyone be resurrected or will only righteous people be?

4. WHEN I AM REVERENT, I SHOW RESPECT FOR JESUS

Jesus was in a boat with his apostles. He decided to rest. But while he was sleeping, a storm came up. The apostles were afraid the boat was going to sink. They woke Jesus up and asked him to help. Jesus told them not to be afraid. He calmed the storm, commanding the waves and winds to be still.

The apostles were amazed at how quickly the storm stopped. They knew Jesus had great power, but they couldn't believe even the winds and waves would obey him. The waves and winds obeyed Jesus because he created them. He is their Master just as he is our Master. The difference between us and things in nature is that we get to choose if we will obey Jesus or not. He will never force us to obey him. But we can show him how much we love and respect him by being still and calm when we visit his house. Being reverent at church helps us to learn more while we are there and feel closer to Jesus.

Thought Question: Can you think of a time when you felt the Spirit at church? What was that like?

SCRIPTURE

And they feared exceedingly, and said one to another, What manner of man is this, that even the wind and the sea obey him? —Mark 4:41

VISUAL AID

GAB 40
"Jesus Calms the Storm"

ILLUSTRATION IDEAS

Jesus, a boat, a storm, a calm sea, a person being reverent

CHAPTER 4

My FAMILY CAN Be TOGETHER FOREVER

"Marriage between a man and a woman is ordained of God and . . . the family is central to the Creator's plan for the eternal destiny of His children." —*The Family: A Proclamation to the World*

1. HEAVENLY FATHER'S PLAN IS ABOUT FAMILIES

SCRIPTURE

And as I partook of the fruit thereof it filled my soul with exceedingly great joy; wherefore, I began to be desirous that my family should partake of it also.
—1 Nephi 8:12

VISUAL AID

GAB 1
"Jesus Christ"

ILLUSTRATION IDEAS

Jesus, the earth, a family, the temple

Before we were born, we lived in heaven with God. There Jesus presented a plan to all of us. Jesus said that we would come to earth and learn to make good choices so that someday we could return to heaven and live there with God again after we died. We all wanted to follow Jesus's plan. The most important part of this plan was that while we were on the earth, we would be part of a family. We need our families to teach us how to choose the right and to keep us safe.

Think about all the things your family helps you with. You need your family, and your family needs you. You could help your family to follow Jesus's plan by learning about your ancestors and preparing to go to the temple someday. You can also help your family choose the right by being a good example.

Thought Question: Do you think Heavenly Father sent you to your family for a reason?

2. PARENTS SHOULD TAKE CARE OF A FAMILY

Mother birds spend a long time sitting on their eggs to keep them warm. Then, when it's time for the eggs to hatch, the mother watches patiently as her babies figure out how to crack open their eggs. While the baby birds are still little, their mother gathers food for them and feeds them in the nest. And once they're old enough, she teaches them how to fly.

Human parents take care of their babies too. Heavenly Father has said that parents are supposed to take good care of their children, both physically and spiritually. This means that your parents should take care of your body by making sure you have enough food to eat and clothes to wear. And they should take care of your spirit by teaching you about Jesus and how to feel the Holy Ghost so you know how to choose the right.

Thought Question: What could you do today that will help you to be a good parent someday?

SCRIPTURE

Parents have a sacred duty to rear their children in love and righteousness, to provide for their physical and spiritual needs.
—*The Family: A Proclamation to the World*, paragraph 6

VISUAL AID

GAB 5
"Adam and Eve Teaching Their Children"

ILLUSTRATION IDEAS

A bird, eggs, a nest, a baby, a mommy and daddy, clothes, food, Jesus

3. I SHOULD OBEY MY PARENTS

SCRIPTURE

Honour thy father and thy mother; that thy days may be long upon the land.
—Exodus 20:12

VISUAL AID

GAB 14
"The Ten Commandments"

ILLUSTRATION IDEAS

A TV and computer, a plate of food, the Ten Commandments, a mommy and daddy, Heavenly Father

At McKenzee's house there are a lot of rules. There are rules about how long you can watch TV or play on the computer. There are rules about what you can and can't eat for dinner. And there are rules about when your chores need to be done. Sometimes it seems to McKenzee like there are so many rules she can't even keep track of them all. McKenzee does her best to follow the rules, but sometimes she makes mistakes.

It's okay to make mistakes sometimes, but we should all try our best to follow the rules. We might not always like them, but rules keep us happy and safe. Parents make rules because they want their kids to learn. Heavenly Father does the same thing. He gives us rules called commandments so that we can learn how to return to him. One of Heavenly Father's commandments is to obey your parents. So when you follow your parents' rules, you are obeying them and Heavenly Father at the same time!

Thought Question: How does your attitude about rules affect the way you obey them?

4. MY FAMILY NEEDS MY LOVE

Some people have big families, and some have small families. Ruth's family was very small. After Ruth's husband died, the only people in Ruth's family were Ruth and her mother-in-law, Naomi. One day, Naomi decided to go back to her homeland. She told Ruth she was leaving, but Ruth wanted to go with her. Ruth loved Naomi because Naomi was part of her family. So Ruth and Naomi traveled to Naomi's home and lived there together.

We need to love our family members too. Whether we have big families or little families, we need to show the people in our families that we love them. We can show our love by doing nice things and by being obedient, respectful, and kind. We also need to tell the people in our families that we love them.

Thought Question: How do the people in your family show their love for each other?

SCRIPTURE

So Naomi returned, and Ruth the Moabitess, her daughter in law, with her.
—Ruth 1:22

VISUAL AID

GAB 17
"Ruth Gleaning in the Fields"

ILLUSTRATION IDEAS

Ruth, Naomi, a heart, a family

CHAPTER 5

PROPHETS TEACH FAMILIES *How* *to* BE HAPPY

"Be mindful of the words which were spoken before
by the holy prophets." —2 Peter 3:2

1. PROPHETS SPEAK FOR HEAVENLY FATHER

SCRIPTURE

By the Spirit are all things made known unto the prophets, which shall come upon the children of men according to the flesh.
—1 Nephi 22:2

VISUAL AID

GAB 137
"Thomas S. Monson"

ILLUSTRATION IDEAS

A girl, a soccer ball, a coach, the prophet, Heavenly Father

Millie likes to play soccer. She knows that when she's playing she needs to listen to her coach and do what she says. Millie's soccer coach has played soccer herself, so she always has good advice. Her coach can also see how the whole game is going. Millie can only see what's happening on her part of the field. Millie has learned that she needs to trust the things that her coach tells her and do her best to follow the coach's instructions.

Each one of us has someone who can be like a coach for us. This person is our prophet. Because they communicate with Heavenly Father, prophets can see things that we can't see on our own. Prophets tell us how to live so that we can be happy. They know how to follow Jesus because they do it themselves. We need to learn to listen to our prophet so that we can hear what he is telling us to do. Listening to the prophet is so important because it's like listening to Heavenly Father.

Thought Question: Why do we only have one prophet instead of lots of prophets?

2. THE PROPHETS IN THE SCRIPTURES TEACH US HOW TO HAVE HAPPY FAMILIES

Do you have a scripture hero? Many people think of Nephi, Moroni, or Joseph Smith as scripture heroes. These men were righteous and heroic, but they couldn't have done everything they did without the help of some very important people—their families.

Nephi taught his brothers how to understand the scriptures. Moroni and his father wrote letters to encourage each other. And Joseph Smith relied on his family to help him spread the news about the true gospel.

We can follow the example of these scripture heroes by loving and serving the people in our family. Families are so important to Heavenly Father. He knows that we will only be happy forever if we can be with our families. That's why he told the prophets in the scriptures what to say to us so that we can make good choices that will help us live with our families eternally.

Thought Question: What other scripture prophets can you think of? What did they teach us about having a happy family?

SCRIPTURE

My beloved son, Moroni . . . I am mindful of you always in my prayers, continually praying unto God . . . that he, through his infinite goodness and grace, will keep you through the endurance of faith on his name to the end.
—Moroni 8:2–3

VISUAL AID

GAB 71
"Lehi and His People Arrive in the Promised Land"

ILLUSTRATION IDEAS

Nephi, Moroni, Joseph Smith, the scriptures, a family, Heavenly Father

3. WHEN MY FAMILY FOLLOWS THE PROPHET, WE ARE BLESSED

SCRIPTURE

Bring ye all the tithes into the storehouse, that there may be meat in mine house . . . and all nations shall call you blessed.
—Malachi 3:10

VISUAL AID

GAB 113
"Payment of Tithing"

ILLUSTRATION IDEAS

A girl, a restaurant, cans of food, the prophet, money, a school

Greta's dad used to go to work every day, but right now he doesn't. Greta knows her dad wants to go back to work. He is looking for a new job. But for now Greta's family has made some changes. Instead of going out to eat dinner at a restaurant, they stay home every night and use the extra food they have in their food storage.

Having food storage is one way to follow the prophet. Prophets teach us to be ready for the future by paying our tithing, storing extra food, and saving money. They also teach us to be kind to others, to go to school and learn as much as we can, and to be careful about what we watch and listen to.

Greta's family is grateful that they followed the prophet by paying their tithing and saving food and money. When we follow the prophet, we are always blessed.

Thought Question: Has your family ever been blessed for following the prophet?

4. GENERAL CONFERENCE IS A SPECIAL TIME TO LISTEN TO THE PROPHET

King Benjamin was the king of all the Nephites. He wanted to tell his people some important things about the gospel, so he planned a special meeting. All of his people brought their tents to the meeting so they could stay and listen. This meeting was a lot like the general conferences we have today. General conference is a special time. It only happens twice a year. We don't bring tents and camp at Temple Square, but we do try to prepare for general conference. We try to make sure we aren't doing anything on those days, and we think about questions we might have about the Church or our lives.

We are so blessed to have living prophets to guide us. And we are blessed when we listen to them reverently during conference and then try to do what they say.

Thought Question: If you were asked to speak at general conference, what would you talk about?

SCRIPTURE

And it came to pass that when they came up to the temple, they pitched their tents round about, every man according to his family. —Mosiah 2:5

VISUAL AID

GAB 74
"King Benjamin Addresses His People"

ILLUSTRATION IDEAS

King Benjamin, the Nephites, tents, a tower, the prophet, the conference center, a TV and computer, the *Ensign*

CHAPTER 6

GOD'S POWER *Can* BLESS *My* FAMILY

"Whatsoever ye shall bind on earth shall be bound in heaven." —Matthew 18:18

1. THE PRIESTHOOD HELPS MY FAMILY

SCRIPTURE

And this greater priesthood administereth the gospel . . . therefore, in the ordinances thereof, the power of godliness is manifest.
—Doctrine and Covenants 84:19–20

VISUAL AID

GAB 107
"Blessing the Sacrament"

ILLUSTRATION IDEAS

A boy, a tree, a dad, Jesus, Heavenly Father

One time Oliver was climbing trees with his cousins, Louisa and Jane. They were having a great time. But then Louisa slipped and fell from a high branch. Her leg was broken. Oliver watched while his dad gave Louisa a blessing. He blessed Louisa that she would be okay. Then they took her to the hospital.

Oliver knew Louisa would be all right because his dad had said so in the blessing. Oliver's dad holds the priesthood. The priesthood is the same power Jesus used to perform miracles while he was alive. Someday Oliver will be able to hold the priesthood too. Having the priesthood is a great responsibility, but it is also a great privilege. We are so blessed to have God's power here on the earth. Without the priesthood, we would not be able to perform all of the ordinances that we need to do here in order to return to Heavenly Father someday.

Thought Question: Is the priesthood important for girls too or just boys?

2. FAMILIES ARE SEALED TOGETHER FOREVER IN THE TEMPLE

Yesterday was a special day for Gracie because she and her brother, Gavin, went to the temple. Their mommy was sealed to her new husband, and then Gracie and Gavin were sealed to both of them.

When they got to the temple, Gracie and Gavin played in a special room and watched a movie about the temple. Then it was time to get ready. Gracie put on her pretty white dress and helped Gavin put on his white suit. While they were in the temple, they walked slowly and spoke quietly because they knew that the temple is Heavenly Father's house. After they were done, they went outside and took lots of pictures so they could remember this day for a long time.

The temple lets every family be sealed together forever. That's why temples are so important. They make it possible for our whole family to be together forever.

Thought Question: Can you still feel the Spirit when you go to the temple even if you can't go inside?

SCRIPTURE

And whatsoever thou shalt bind on earth shall be bound in heaven.
—Matthew 16:19

VISUAL AID

GAB 119
"Salt Lake Temple"

ILLUSTRATION IDEAS

A girl, the temple, a white dress, a camera, Heavenly Father

3. SOMEDAY I WILL GO TO THE TEMPLE

SCRIPTURE

Organize yourselves; prepare every needful thing, and establish a house; even a house of prayer, a house of fasting, a house of faith, a house of learning, a house of glory, a house of order, a house of God.
—Doctrine and Covenants 109:8

VISUAL AID

GAB 101
"Mary Fielding Smith and Joseph F. Smith Crossing the Plains"

ILLUSTRATION IDEAS

Pioneers, houses, stones, a temple, Heavenly Father

When the pioneers reached Salt Lake City, one of the first things they did was start building a temple. It took them forty years to finish. Stone by stone they worked. They made many sacrifices for the temple.

Someday each of us can go to the temple. But just like it took the pioneers a long time to build the temple in Salt Lake, it takes us a long time to get ready to go inside the temple. You can start preparing now, while you are still young, to go to the temple. It may take a lot of hard work and sacrifice to be able to enter the temple, but it is worth it. In the temple, you can feel so close to Heavenly Father. He will help you to prepare yourself to enter the temple because he wants you to come and be with him there.

Thought Question: What kinds of things do you need to do or not do in order to be worthy to go to the temple?

4. I CAN LEARN ABOUT MY ANCESTORS

Think about all the people in your family. Do you have brothers and sisters? Do you have grandparents? What about great-grandparents? What about your great-grandparents' great-grandparents? These people are called your ancestors.

Your family members who are alive love you. The ones who have already died love you too. Even though you can't see them or talk to them right now, they are still your family. They want you to make good choices so you can all be together forever.

You can learn about your family by talking with your parents, looking at old journals and other records, and preparing to go to the temple someday so you can be baptized for people who have already died.

Thought Question: What are some names of your ancestors? Do you know any stories about them?

SCRIPTURE

And he shall turn the heart of the fathers to the children, and the heart of the children to their fathers.
—Malachi 4:6

VISUAL AID

GAB 121
"Temple Baptismal Font"

ILLUSTRATION IDEAS

A group of people, a family, journals, the temple

CHAPTER 7

I NEED *to* BE BAPTIZED *and* CONFIRMED

"Except a man be born of water and of the Spirit, he cannot enter into the kingdom of God." —John 3:5

1. JOSEPH SMITH RESTORED THE CHURCH OF JESUS CHRIST

SCRIPTURE

We believe in the same organization that existed in the primitive church.
—Articles of Faith 1:6

VISUAL AID

GAB 92
"Joseph Smith Translating the Book of Mormon"

ILLUSTRATION IDEAS

An old machine, tools, Joseph Smith, a church building

What does it mean to restore something? When we restore furniture or machines, we take something that is old and clean and fix it until it works like new again. This means that something that has been restored is both old and new at the same time. The same is true for our church.

Joseph Smith wanted to know which church was right. So he prayed. Heavenly Father and Jesus visited him and told him that the churches around him were not working anymore. Instead, Joseph would need to restore the true Church. He did this by following the revelations and promptings Jesus gave him.

Now we have a church that is both old and new. It is old because it is the same church that was on the earth long ago. But it is also a new church because it works like new. Just like in older times, our church still helps us learn about Jesus and it teaches us how to return to him.

Thought Question: What specific things in our church were restored through Joseph Smith?

2. I JOIN THE CHURCH WHEN I AM BAPTIZED AND CONFIRMED

Leo's mom didn't used to go to church. His dad had been baptized a long time ago, but he had stopped going to church too. Then one day the missionaries came to visit Leo's parents. The missionaries asked if they could teach Leo's mom. She said yes. In time, the missionaries invited Leo's mom to be baptized. Leo's mom believed that the church was true. She wanted Leo to know the truth too. She decided to be baptized.

Their whole family began going to church together. Now that Leo is almost eight, he is excited to be baptized and confirmed just like his mom was. When we are baptized, we become members of the Church. We promise to help each other and to look out for one another. We also receive the Holy Ghost. The Holy Ghost helps us to know the truth. Leo is happy that someday soon he will become a member of the Church just like his parents.

Thought Question: Why do we need to be baptized?

SCRIPTURE

Behold, baptism is unto repentance to the fulfilling the commandments unto the remission of sins. —Moroni 8:11

VISUAL AID

GAB 103 "Young Man Being Baptized"

ILLUSTRATION IDEAS

A boy, a mom and dad, missionaries, a baptismal font, the Holy Ghost

3. THE HOLY GHOST HELPS ME WHEN I'M SAD OR CONFUSED

SCRIPTURE

And because of meekness and lowliness of heart cometh the visitation of the Holy Ghost, which Comforter filleth with hope and perfect love.
—Moroni 8:26

VISUAL AID

GAB 105
"The Gift of the Holy Ghost"

ILLUSTRATION IDEAS

A girl, a fair, the Holy Ghost, Jesus, Heavenly Father, a smile

One time Amelia went to the fair with her family. She had a lot of fun looking at the animals and riding on the rides. But then something bad happened: Amelia got lost. She was scared. She couldn't see her family anywhere. And she didn't know what to do. Amelia started to cry.

Then she remembered something she should do. She said a prayer and asked Heavenly Father to help her not to be scared. As she finished her prayer, Amelia felt peaceful and calm. She knew that it was the Holy Ghost. The Holy Ghost is called "the Comforter." He works with Jesus and Heavenly Father to keep us safe, help us when we need help, and cheer us up when we're sad.

When Amelia's family found her, she told them all about her prayer. Her family was glad that Amelia was safe, and they were also glad she had felt the peace that comes from the Holy Ghost.

Thought Question: How can the Holy Ghost be everywhere at the same time?

4. THE HOLY GHOST ALWAYS TELLS THE TRUTH

Korihor said that Jesus and Heavenly Father were not real. When Alma found out about this, he was upset. Alma knew that Jesus and Heavenly Father were real because an angel had appeared to him. Alma asked Korihor why he was telling lies. Korihor said he would stop if God gave him some sort of sign. So God took away Korihor's voice so that Korihor couldn't lie anymore. Later Korihor admitted that he had been lying. He said that Satan had appeared to him. Satan had told Korihor those lies. Then Korihor repeated them to the people around him.

We can know if something is true or if it's a lie when we listen to the Holy Ghost. The Holy Ghost always tells the truth. He will never lie. In fact, he couldn't lie even if he wanted to. When you know the truth, it will be much harder for Satan to tell you lies like the ones he told Korihor.

Thought Question: The Holy Ghost speaks to each of us in different ways. What does it feel like when the Holy Ghost speaks to you?

SCRIPTURE

The Holy Ghost . . . shall teach you all things and bring all things to your remembrance, whatsoever I have said unto you.
—John 14:26

VISUAL AID

GAB 77
"Conversion of Alma the Younger"

ILLUSTRATION IDEAS

Korihor, Alma, the Holy Ghost, a question mark

CHAPTER 8

MY FAMILY *Can* WORK *and* PLAY TOGETHER

"Successful . . . families are established and maintained on principles of faith, prayer, repentance, forgiveness, respect, love, compassion, work, and wholesome recreational activities." —*The Family: A Proclamation to the World*

1. PRAYING TOGETHER BLESSES MY FAMILY

SCRIPTURE

Pray in your families unto the Father, always in my name, that your wives and your children may be blessed.
—3 Nephi 18:21

VISUAL AID

GAB 112
"Family Prayer"

ILLUSTRATION IDEAS

A girl, a boy, a teddy bear, a tree, a mommy, Jesus, a family praying together

Lucas is Hayden's little brother. He's only two years old. Lucas loves to say prayers, and when he does, he prays for everything. He prays for his trucks and teddy bears. He prays for the trees outside and their pet goldfish. He even prays for the carpet and the windows and the broom. Lucas's prayers used to make Hayden laugh. Then their mommy explained that Lucas was still learning how to pray and that it was important for Hayden to be reverent. Hayden's mommy said that Jesus listens to every prayer, even if the person praying is only two years old.

The important thing is that Hayden's family says prayers together. When they pray together, everyone in her family feels more love and peace. Saying prayers helps Hayden, Lucas, their sister, and their parents to remember Jesus and Heavenly Father. This helps them all to be happier.

Thought Question: Has your family ever prayed and fasted together for something important?

2. MY FAMILY GROWS STRONGER WHEN WE HAVE FAMILY HOME EVENING

Every family is different. Some families have two parents, and some have one. Some families have one kid, and others have a lot more than that. Some families live with grandparents, aunts, uncles, or cousins. No matter how many people are in a family, every family will be blessed for having family home evening.

Family home evening is a special time for a family to be together. But just like every family is different, every family home evening is different too. Some families like to have a lesson and an activity for family home evening. Some like to watch a church movie. Others read stories or play games. And other families go to parks, play sports together, or do craft projects.

That's okay. In fact, the prophets have told us that it doesn't really matter what you do for family home evening as long as you take some time to be together and try to feel the Spirit.

Thought Question: What are some of your favorite memories of family home evening?

SCRIPTURE

Successful marriages and families are established and maintained on principles of faith, prayer, repentance, forgiveness, respect, love, compassion, work, and wholesome recreational activities.
—*The Family: A Proclamation to the World*

VISUAL AID

GAB 137
"Thomas S. Monson"

ILLUSTRATION IDEAS

A family, a movie, a book, a park, the prophet, a smile

And we had obtained the records which the Lord had commanded us, and searched them and found that they were . . . of great worth unto us, insomuch that we could preserve the commandments of the Lord unto our children.
—1 Nephi 5:21

VISUAL AID

GAB 73
"Mormon Abridging the Plates"

ILLUSTRATION IDEAS

Nephi, the brass plates, the scriptures, a family, a smile

3. READING THE SCRIPTURES KEEPS MY FAMILY CLOSE TO CHRIST

Nephi's family knew how powerful the scriptures are. After they left Jerusalem, Nephi and his brothers went back to get the brass plates. The brass plates contained the scriptures and other important things that Nephi's family needed to help them on their journey to the promised land. Once they made it to the promised land, Nephi and his family kept reading from the brass plates. The brass plates helped Nephi's children to stay good even when the people around them were being wicked.

The scriptures we have today are just as powerful as the brass plates. When you read the scriptures with your family, you can talk about the gospel and learn from each other. The things you read and talk about will help you, your parents, and everyone you love. The power that comes from the scriptures can keep your whole family happy and safe.

Thought Question: Does it matter when your family reads the scriptures or how you study them?

4. SUNDAY IS A SPECIAL DAY TO REST AND WORSHIP

Working hard is important. Many people think it is the most important thing in the world. For other people the most important thing is having fun. They are always thinking about new fun things to do. While it is important to work hard and to have fun, neither of these are the most important thing in the world.

Heavenly Father taught us what is most important. When he and Jesus created the earth, they worked hard for six days. Then on the seventh day, they rested. This was an example to each of us. We are supposed to work hard and play hard every day except on Sundays. Sundays are a time to remember that the most important things are the things that bring us closer to Heavenly Father. On Sundays we can rest from our work and our play. Instead of focusing on ourselves, we can focus on Heavenly Father and others. That is how we show him that we love him more than anything else in the world.

Thought Question: Who decides what sorts of things you can and can't do on Sunday?

SCRIPTURE

Keep the sabbath day to sanctify it, as the Lord thy God hath commanded thee. —Deuteronomy 5:12

VISUAL AID

GAB 108
"Passing the Sacrament"

ILLUSTRATION IDEAS

A person working, a person having fun, Jesus, Heavenly Father

CHAPTER 9

My FAMILY Can CHOOSE the RIGHT

"We believe in being honest, true, chaste, benevolent, virtuous, and in doing good to all men; indeed, we may say that we follow the admonition of Paul—We believe all things, we hope all things, we have endured many things, and hope to be able to endure all things. If there is anything virtuous, lovely, or of good report or praiseworthy, we seek after these things." —Articles of Faith 1:13

1. SAYING THANK YOU SHOWS I'M GRATEFUL

SCRIPTURE

And he who receiveth all things with thankfulness shall be made glorious; and the things of this earth shall be added unto him.
—Doctrine and Covenants 78:19

VISUAL AID

GAB 2
"The Lord Created All Things"

ILLUSTRATION IDEAS

A girl, some crafts, clouds, a tree, a heart, Heavenly Father

One of Diana's favorite things is to make crafts. She works hard to create things that are perfect. And when she's done, she's always excited to show them to her friends and family. Sometimes she gives the things she makes to other people as presents. Diana feels great when they tell her "thank you" for the things she makes.

Heavenly Father likes to create things too. Sometimes he creates things we can see and touch, like beautiful clouds, ocean waves, or strong trees. Sometimes the things he creates are not visible. These are things like love and peace. We need to make sure we thank Heavenly Father for all of the things he creates for us. Heavenly Father loves it when we notice the things he creates and when we are grateful for them. When we pray, we can tell Heavenly Father how much we love the things he makes and how thankful we are to have them.

Thought Question: Besides Heavenly Father, who else makes things for you? How can you show that you are thankful for the things people make?

2. WHEN I SERVE OTHERS, I SERVE GOD

Someday soon, Jason will hold the priesthood. He is excited to help pass the sacrament and to be in the deacons quorum instead of going to primary. Jason knows the priesthood is the same power Heavenly Father uses. This means that when Jason or anyone else uses the priesthood, that person is doing something that Heavenly Father would do. That person is acting in place of Heavenly Father.

The priesthood is wonderful, but we don't need to have the priesthood in order to act in Heavenly Father's place. Anytime you serve someone else, you are doing something that Heavenly Father would do if he were here. And because of this, every time you give service to others, you are also giving service to Heavenly Father. You can give service by being a good friend, doing some extra chores, or writing a note to someone who is sick or sad. Serving others will make you happy because you will know Heavenly Father is pleased with you and that he loves you and everyone you serve.

Thought Question: How do you feel when someone serves you? Do you try to make it easy or hard for people to do things for you?

SCRIPTURE

When ye are in the service of your fellow beings ye are only in the service of your God.
—Mosiah 2:17

VISUAL AID

GAB 106
"Ordination to the Priesthood"

ILLUSTRATION IDEAS

A boy, a person giving service, a note, Heavenly Father, a smile

3. I CAN BE HONEST

SCRIPTURE

For I had seen a vision; I knew it, and I knew that God knew it, and I could not deny it, neither dared I do it.
—Joseph Smith—
History 1:25

VISUAL AID

GAB 89
"Joseph Smith Seeks Wisdom in the Bible"

ILLUSTRATION IDEAS

Joseph Smith, a group of people, Jesus, Heavenly Father

After Joseph Smith saw Heavenly Father and Jesus Christ, he told his family and friends. Some of them believed him, but some of them did not. Many of Joseph's neighbors were angry with him. They thought he wasn't telling the truth. But Joseph Smith knew what he had seen. He could not deny what had really happened or he would be lying to himself and to God.

We need to be honest like Joseph was. It can be hard to tell the truth, especially when it makes other people angry. But Joseph Smith knew that the most important thing is not what other people think of us. The most important thing is what Heavenly Father thinks of us. Heavenly Father knows when we are honest, even if know one else knows. He will always bless us when we tell the truth.

Thought Question: What does it mean to live with integrity?

4. I CAN BE A LIGHT TO OTHERS

When Jesus lived on the earth, he wanted to teach his followers to be good examples for all the other people around them. He told the people that they were like a light. He told them that they needed to shine brightly so that the people around them would be able to see the truth. When we have light, we can see which way is the right way.

You can be a light for the people around you by choosing the right. When they see you making a good choice and how happy you are, they will want to make good choices too. Your example will help others to see the truth about the gospel, just as if you were holding up a flashlight or a candle in a dark place. That's why it's so important for us not to be afraid to make good choices, no matter what. You need to choose the right when lots of people are watching and when it seems like no one will notice.

Your example and light will lead others to the truth so that they can be happy, just like you.

Thought Question: Who are some people that you look up to as good examples? Why do you look up to them?

SCRIPTURE

Let your light so shine before men, that they may see your good works, and glorify your Father which is in heaven.
—Matthew 5:14

VISUAL AID

GAB 61
"Go Ye Therefore"

ILLUSTRATION IDEAS

Jesus, a flashlight, a candle, darkness, a smile

CHAPTER 10

The FAMILY PROCLAMATION BLESSES My FAMILY

"These things have I spoken unto you, that my joy might remain in you, and that your joy might be full." —John 15:11

1. THE FAMILY PROCLAMATION IS FOR MY FAMILY

SCRIPTURE

The pointers which were in the ball . . . did work according to the faith and diligence and heed which we did give unto them.
—1 Nephi 16:28

VISUAL AID

GAB 68
"The Liahona"

ILLUSTRATION IDEAS

Lehi, the Liahona, the family proclamation, the earth, Heavenly Father

When Lehi's family was traveling through the wilderness, Heavenly Father wanted to make sure they knew which way to go. He gave Lehi a special tool called the "Liahona," which pointed the way they should go. It also had writing on it, which taught Lehi what to do and how to lead his family. But the Liahona only worked when Lehi's family obeyed what it said and followed the directions from the Lord.

Today we have a special tool to help our families. This tool is called "The Family: A Proclamation to the World." The proclamation came from Heavenly Father, just like the Liahona. If we follow its teachings, our families will be blessed. But it will only work for us if we do what it says. We should follow the family proclamation because it teaches us how to be a happy family here on earth and eternally.

Thought Question: The family proclamation teaches some important eternal truths that many people today don't understand. Do you know what these are? Do you know why they are so important?

2. MARRIAGE IS PART OF GOD'S PLAN

Rebekah was a righteous young woman. One evening while she was at a well, she met a man who asked her for water. Rebekah gave the man water for himself and all his camels. Later Rebekah found out that Abraham had sent the man at the well to find a wife for Abraham's son, Isaac. Abraham and Isaac were righteous men. Rebekah chose to marry Isaac because she knew it was what Heavenly Father wanted her to do.

Many things have changed since Rebekah was alive. But things like marriage have stayed the same. Through his prophets, Heavenly Father has told us how important it is to find someone righteous to marry in the temple. And he has told us that marriage is meant for a man and a woman. Though many things in our world change, we can be sure that the important things about marriage, families, and Heavenly Father's plan will always be the same. That's because Heavenly Father loves each of us and he knows what will make us happy now and eternally.

Thought Question: What kind of person do you want to be when you get married? How can you prepare to become that person?

SCRIPTURE

And Isaac . . . took Rebekah, and she became his wife; and he loved her.
—Genesis 24:67

VISUAL AID

GAB 10
"Rebekah at the Well"

ILLUSTRATION IDEAS

Rebekah, Isaac, the prophet, the temple, a bride and groom

57

3. JESUS TAUGHT US HOW TO HAVE HAPPY FAMILIES

SCRIPTURE

Thou shalt love the Lord thy God. . . . This is the first and great commandment. And the second is like unto it, Thou shalt love thy neighbor as thyself.
—Matthew 22:37–39

VISUAL AID

GAB 39
"The Sermon on the Mount"

ILLUSTRATION IDEAS

A boy, a mommy and daddy, a toy, a bed, Jesus, a smile

Jesus said that the most important commandment is to love God and the people around us. Henry knows that some of the people around him are the people in his own family. Henry loves his family. He tries to show his love by listening to his parents and doing what they say. Jesus also taught us to share with others, so Henry shares his toys with his little sister. Jesus taught us to look for ways to help other people. Henry tries to help his family by doing chores.

Some people think that Jesus only taught us how to be good people on our own. They don't understand that everything Jesus taught was to show us how to be happy in our families. Jesus wants us to be part of a family. It is only when we are sealed together as families that we can be happy eternally. Henry's family is trying to do the things Jesus taught so that they can be happy now and stay together forever.

Thought Question: Can you list some of the things Jesus taught while he was on the earth? How do these teachings relate to your family?

4. MY FAMILY WORKS TOGETHER

Paul taught that the Church is like a body. Each church member has a different role to play, just like each part of the body does something different. Our families are the same. Each person in your family has a special role to play, and special things only he or she can add to your family. Just like a hand is different from an eye and a nose is different from a heart, each person in a family is different too.

Heavenly Father sent you to your family because he knew you would be able to help your family. He also knew they would be able to help you. When you and your family work together, you can do great things. Working as a family will show you how each person helps in his or her own way, just like each part of your body does something different but equally important.

Thought Question: Why does Heavenly Father want us to learn how to work?

SCRIPTURE

If the whole body were an eye, where were the hearing? . . . But now hath God set the members every one of them in the body, as it hath pleased him.
—1 Corinthians 12:17

VISUAL AID

GAB 115
"Service"

ILLUSTRATION IDEAS

Paul, a hand, an eye, a nose, a heart, a family

CHAPTER 11

JESUS TAUGHT ME and MY FAMILY HOW to LIVE

"Happiness in family life is most likely to be achieved when founded upon the teachings of the Lord Jesus Christ." —*The Family: A Proclamation to the World*

1. HAVING FAITH BLESSES MY FAMILY

SCRIPTURE

And it came to pass that the brother of Jared did cry unto the Lord, and the Lord had compassion upon their friends and their families also, that they were not confounded.
—Ether 1:37

VISUAL AID

GAB 85
"The Brother of Jared Sees the Finger of the Lord"

ILLUSTRATION IDEAS

Jared, Jared's brother, a person praying, Heavenly Father, a family

Jared and his brother were righteous, but the people around them were not. Heavenly Father wanted to teach these people a lesson, so he confused their language and made it so that the people couldn't talk to each other. Jared and his brother wanted their family to be able to stay together and talk to each other. Jared asked his brother to pray. Their family had faith that if Jared's brother prayed, Heavenly Father would hear him and answer his prayer.

Heavenly Father did hear Jared's brother. Because they were righteous and had faith, Jared's family got to stay together and they could still talk to each other. In time, Heavenly Father led their family to a promised land where they could live together and be blessed.

Your family will also be blessed by your faith. You can show your faith by praying and obeying the commandments. When you do these things, Heavenly Father will bless you and your whole family.

Thought Question: Why is faith the first principle of the gospel?

2. I TALK TO GOD WHEN I PRAY

Charity's grandparents are serving a mission in Buenos Aires, Argentina. Charity likes to send them pictures and letters in the mail. Her parents read her the emails they send home. And sometimes they get to talk on the phone or online. It's always fun when Charity gets to see her grandparents or hear their voices. She loves them and misses them.

Heavenly Father loves and misses us too. While we are here on earth, it's sort of like we are all serving long missions. We have to be away from our Heavenly Father during our earthly missions, but we can still talk to him when we pray. Heavenly Father always wants to know what we're doing and how he can help us. That's why he has told us we need to pray always.

Thought Question: What kinds of things should we talk about with Heavenly Father when we pray?

SCRIPTURE

Let your hearts be full, drawn out in prayer unto him continually for your welfare, and also for the welfare of those who are around you.
—Alma 34:27

VISUAL AID

GAB 111
"Young Boy Praying"

ILLUSTRATION IDEAS

A girl, a grandma and grandpa, a letter, a computer, Heavenly Father

3. I CAN CHANGE MY MIND AND HEART

SCRIPTURE

The Spirit of the Lord . . . has wrought a mighty change in us, or in our hearts, that we have no more disposition to do evil, but to do good continually.
—Mosiah 5:2

VISUAL AID

GAB 56
"Jesus Praying in Gethsemane"

ILLUSTRATION IDEAS

A girl, a fireman, a princess, Jesus, a heart, a smile

Morgan loves to play dress up. She has lots of costumes. She has a firefighter outfit, a princess dress, a pirate costume, and a superhero cape. But no matter what costume Morgan is wearing, she is still the same person on the inside. Many people think they can change who they are on the inside by changing things like their clothes, where they live, or what they do for fun.

We know that the quickest way to change who you are is to use the Atonement. The Atonement is the sacrifice Jesus made for us when he died. You use the Atonement to repent when you make a mistake. But you can also use it to help you become a better person. That's because the Atonement can change how you think and feel about something. It works on your mind and in your heart. With the Atonement, you can become exactly the person that Heavenly Father wants you to be.

Thought Question: What does Heavenly Father require from us in order for us to use the Atonement?

4. PEACE COMES FROM FORGIVING AND BEING FORGIVEN

Job was a righteous man and Heavenly Father blessed him for being good. Then Job lost his home, his family, and his money. He also got sick. Job's friends told him he should be angry with God. But Job knew being angry wouldn't help anything and would only make him feel worse.

Sometimes when bad things happen, it can make us angry—especially when it's someone else's fault. But Jesus knows what is fair and he will work it out. So instead of getting angry, we need to forgive other people when they make mistakes so that Heavenly Father will forgive us when we make mistakes.

You should remember to forgive yourself too. When you make a mistake, you should repent. Then you should stop worrying about the mistake you made and trust Jesus to make things right. Learning how to forgive and be forgiven can be hard at first, but it is the only way to feel real peace.

Thought Question: Have you ever had a hard time forgiving someone? How did you feel when you finally did forgive that person?

SCRIPTURE

The Lord gave, and the Lord hath taken away; blessed be the name of the Lord.
—Job 1:21

VISUAL AID

GAB 60
"Jesus Shows His Wounds"

ILLUSTRATION IDEAS

Job, a house, a family, money, Jesus, a smile

CHAPTER 12

I Can REMEMBER JESUS, My SAVIOR

"Jesus saith unto him, I am the way, the truth, and the life: no man cometh unto the Father, but by me." —John 14:6

1. I THINK OF JESUS DURING THE SACRAMENT

SCRIPTURE

He brake it, and said, Take, eat: this is my body, which is broken for you: this do in remembrance of me.
—1 Corinthians 11:24

VISUAL AID

GAB 54
"The Last Supper"

ILLUSTRATION IDEAS

A Christmas tree, decorations, a star, bread and water, Jesus, the Holy Ghost

The star on a Christmas tree is a symbol. When you see a symbol, it helps you to remember something else. In our church, we use symbols like the Christmas star all year long. We can find symbols at the temple, in the songs we sing, and in the scriptures.

The sacrament is one of those symbols. The bread and water help us remember Jesus's body and his blood. Jesus sacrificed his body and blood for us when he died. When we take the sacrament, we promise to remember Jesus always. Next time you take the sacrament, watch and listen closely. Look for symbols that teach you about Jesus and how he died for you. Your parents and the Holy Ghost can help you find symbols. It's also important to be reverent during the sacrament. When you are reverent, the people around you can find symbols too and you can all remember Jesus together.

Thought Question: What other symbols have you noticed in our church?

2. JESUS HELPS ME CHOOSE THE RIGHT

Taylor loves to do puzzles. She can do really hard ones with hundreds of pieces. One thing Taylor has learned is that while she's working on a puzzle, she needs to look at the picture of what the puzzle will look like when it's finished. Looking at the finished picture helps Taylor figure out which pieces to work on first and where they might go.

If you think about it, Jesus is like a finished puzzle picture. He lived a perfect life. When we look at his life and his example, we can figure out how to live a perfect life too. Whenever you need to make a choice, it's like you're holding a puzzle piece. You could try to figure out what to choose on your own, but that would be like trying to do a puzzle without looking at the picture. None of us can become perfect without Jesus. But if you follow his example and try your best, he will help you with all your choices so that someday, you can become just like him.

Thought Question: Why can't we become perfect on our own?

SCRIPTURE

I am the way, the truth, and the life: no man cometh unto the Father, but by me.
—John 14:6

VISUAL AID

GAB 47
"Christ and the Children"

ILLUSTRATION IDEAS

A girl, a puzzle piece, a puzzle box, Jesus

3. JESUS WAS BORN IN BETHLEHEM

SCRIPTURE

By small and simple things are great things brought to pass; and small means in many instances doth confound the wise.
—Alma 37:6

VISUAL AID

GAB 30
"The Birth of Jesus"

ILLUSTRATION IDEAS

Jesus, a baby, a king, a stable, Heavenly Father

So many people were excited for Jesus to be born. They had looked forward to it for a long time. They wanted to meet their king. But some people were hoping Jesus would make a big entrance. They did not expect him to be born as a little baby in a stable.

Jesus and Heavenly Father knew what would be best. Heavenly Father often uses small and simple things to make great big things happen. When Jesus was born, it seemed like a small thing. But in fact, it was the beginning of a great big thing that would change the whole world forever.

Sometimes you might feel small. You might think the things you do don't matter or make a difference. But remember that Jesus was once small too. Jesus and Heavenly Father love you. They care about all the big and small things you do. As you make small good choices, you can change your life in a big way.

Thought Question: What does it mean when we say that Jesus condescended below all things?

4. SOMEDAY JESUS WILL RETURN

John was one of Jesus's good friends. He was also an apostle. Because he was righteous, John learned many things from Jesus and from the Holy Ghost. He wrote down what he learned. Later John's writings became part of the New Testament. One of the books John wrote is called "Revelation." This book tells us what will happen when Jesus comes again.

John wrote about many signs and wonders that would come before Jesus returned. Some of those signs are already happening. It's exciting to think that Jesus will come back to the earth someday. We can get ready for his return by sharing the gospel with our friends and neighbors. And we can be sure to make good choices so that when Jesus comes, he will be happy to see us and we will be happy to see him. Reading the scriptures, especially books like Revelation, will help us prepare for the day when Jesus will return.

Thought Question: What are some of the signs we can look forward to before Jesus returns?

SCRIPTURE

Behold he cometh with clouds; and every eye shall see him, and they also which pierced him: and all kindreds of the earth shall wail because of him. —Revelation 1:7

VISUAL AID

GAB 66
"The Second Coming"

ILLUSTRATION IDEAS

John, some papers with writing, the scriptures, the earth, Jesus, a smile

Song Ideas

The following is a list of songs from the Children's Songbook that correspond to each talk. You can use them to reinforce the concepts taught in Primary that week. If your musical abilities are limited or you don't have access to an instrument, all of these songs are available at lds.org/music.

CHAPTER 1
1. I Lived in Heaven, 4
   I Will Follow God's Plan, 164
2. He Sent His Son, 34
   I'm Trying to Be like Jesus, 78
3. Beautiful Savior, 62
   Teach Me to Walk in the Light, 177
   Shine On, 144
4. Jesus Once Was a Little Child, 55
   I Feel My Savior's Love, 74

CHAPTER 2

CHAPTER 3

CHAPTER 4

CHAPTER 5

CHAPTER 6

1. The Priesthood Is Restored, 89
   Love Is Spoken Here, 190
2. I Love to See the Temple, 95
   Families Can Be Together Forever, 188
3. The Lord Gave Me a Temple, 153
   I Love to See the Temple, 95
4. Truth from Elijah, 90
   Family History—I Am Doing It, 94

CHAPTER 7

1. On a Golden Springtime, 88, verse 3
   The Priesthood Is Restored, 89
   This Is My Beloved Son, 76, verse 3
2. Baptism, 100
   When I Am Baptized, 103
   The Holy Ghost, 105
3. The Still Small Voice, 106
   Where Love Is, 138
4. Tell Me, Dear Lord, 176
   Search, Ponder, and Pray, 109

CHAPTER 8

CHAPTER 9

CHAPTER 10

CHAPTER 11

CHAPTER 12

About the Author

Heidi Doxey has authored four books in the Tiny Talks series. She lives in the Bay Area, where she currently works as a nanny for one ten-year-old, one eight-year-old, one five-year-old, one four-year-old, four two-year-olds, and a one-year-old—from five different families, so she's never with more than two children at a time. She also enjoys serving in the Oakland Temple and spending time with family and friends. Playing volleyball and soccer, going to the beach, hiking, going for bike rides, cooking, traveling, sewing, gardening, and reading are among the many hobbies she wishes she had more time to pursue.

About the Illustrator

Corey Egbert has always loved books and art, so when he discovered that he could create both at the same time by being an illustrator, he couldn't have been happier. His illustrations can be seen in The Niuhi Shark Saga books, *The Holy Ghost Is like a Blanket*, and the album covers of recording artist Rob Taylor. He lives in Rockbridge County, Virginia, with his wife, Natalya; son, Oliver; and their cat, Rex.